Unfolding In Silence

From Storms to Silent Strength

Rekha Gore

BookLeaf
Publishing

India | USA | UK

Made with ❤ on the BookLeaf Publishing Platform
www.bookleafpub.in
www.bookleafpub.com

Dedication

To the ones who left me in silence, and the ones who made that silence bearable.
To those who doubted me — thank you for teaching me resilience.
And to those who believed in me louder than I believed in myself — your quiet faith kept me breathing.
This is for all of you.

You shaped my words.

Preface

I've always written poems in quiet spaces, like notebook backs and Instagram under #herlyricalheart. Poetry has been my way to feel, breathe, and heal.
When others shared how my poems echoed their emotions, it became a sacred connection. The BookLeaf 21-Day Challenge felt like a sign to make my words lasting.
These poems are born from storms of silence, pain, and hope. If they find you, I hope they feel like home.

— Rekha Gore
insta #herlyricalheart

Acknowledgements

- *To the silent supporters — your quiet appreciation gave my words a place to land, reminding me that even the softest voice is heard.*

- *To those who said, "this feels like me" — thank you for making me feel less alone, and for allowing my poems to hold space for your emotions.*

- *To my son — your love has been my anchor, your strength my guide. This book carries my words, but it also carries your unwavering support. I love you to the Icarus and back.*

Refill When Empty

Refill when empty —
we do that for a glass...
Then why not refill
the joy within our hearts?

Get up from that broken chair,
look around for the light.
Collect what makes you smile —
until you feel just right.

You deserve to be happy.
Don't beg it from someone.
Be kind to *yourself* too —
kindness isn't just for everyone.

Gently guide yourself,
prioritize your own care.
Instead of waiting for help,
be the one who's always there.

Refill when empty —
we do that for a glass...
Then why not refill
the joy within our hearts?

Before I Blame My Face

Mirror, mirror,
where are you?
Can you show me me
before I do something untrue?

Can you make me a kite,
let me rise to the sky?
I want to feel my strength —
my self-doubt is too high.

I keep on affirming
that the universe is kind,
but I never really learned
to treat myself with a gentle mind.

Mirror, mirror,
I need your grace —
show me a sign
when I start blaming my own face.

I can stand strong,
shoulders proudly back —
I can walk straight
with no more zigzag.

Mirror, mirror,
hope your ears are wide —
let's be partners
in rebuilding what I've kept inside.

Break The Silence

The more you stay silent,
the more distance grows.
Take care of your people
before they turn to shadows.

Silence is a storm
that no one can see.
It's easy to stay calm —
communication is the key.

Five golden words
we learned back in school —
used them only for marks,
but forgot their life rule.

In the stillness of a moment,
let's find our voice.
Cherish the kind of love
that makes hearts rejoice.

Happy Swirl

She said she has power
To conquer the world...
But you held her down
And made her dreams swirl.

She exhausted each moment,
She begged you to stop,
Still, you ensured
Every effort would flop.

She raised her arms,
Raised her voice,
Pulled herself out—
Ignoring all noise.

She started from zero,
Maybe even below,
Yet fought with courage,
Letting her true self show.

She left the world's judgment,
Built her own space,
With stars and smiles
She found her place.

Rest Beneath the Night

Once upon a time,
There was a butterfly,
Flying over flowers,
Letting its happiness multiply.

One day, a wasp
Chased it far and long;
Delicate wings grew tired,
Its throat whispered a last song.

A raindrop from nowhere
Offered a spark of hope;
While the wasp wasn't watching,
It dared itself to cope.

Flying far from danger,
It landed on a rock,
Realizing life is fleeting—
A story ticking on a clock.

It watched the sky above,
Felt the breeze so light,
Grateful just to breathe again,
And rest beneath the night.

The Quiet Rebirth

Shhh... don't make a sound,
She just found herself.
Let her enjoy this moment,
As she rearranges each shelf.

Don't make any sound,
She's busy with clearance.
She'll rise strong and shining,
In every next appearance.

Don't make any noise,
She's opening her wings...
So many things falling apart—
Even her marriage ring.

It's pain, it's raw emotion,
Tears may tear her apart...
But what will emerge
Is a beautifully rebuilt heart.

Move On, My dear

Move on from the past
That continues to haunt you.
Move on from the hurt
That still tries to taunt you.

You've got to wake up,
You've got to get up —
The only thing that matters
Is truly *you*, so don't give up.

There's no one out there
Counting the pain you've felt.
No one keeping track
Of the scars you've been dealt.

Don't let your crying
Write tomorrow's tale —
Tears only smudge the ink
And make your vision pale.

Move on, my dear —
Be the hero in your story.
Shatter all that brought you pain.
Be the goddess of your glory.

What Anxiety Feels Like

Hold on my hand,
Just walk with me.
I'm like you all —
Just talk with me.

They say I'm too sensitive,
And maybe that's my shame,
But you've known me forever —
You know I'm not the same.

I'm scared of people,
Tired of the trying,
Sick of seeing myself
With a smile that's lying.

I don't know what I need —
A good morning or just sleep,
To laugh until I break,
Or take a day to weep.

I'm scared of the mirror,
Of a knock on the door,
Of someone calling my name...
What if I don't look like me anymore?

I can't stop my thoughts,
So I stay always busy.
Please don't misunderstand me
If my behavior seems dizzy.

Peace, at Last

She was just a girl,
Dreaming of a place her own—
A quiet little corner,
To call her heart and home.

But the mistake she made
Was letting a mouse inside;
She saw it as harmless,
While it tore her peace with pride.

When truth came to light,
She tried to make him see;
But in giving him a chance,
She lost her own clarity.

She looked up for mercy,
But was met with the cold;
Even those she called her own,
Just watched her story unfold.

She took her last breath
Alone in that deep, dark hole;
And people gathered 'round
To pray for her soul.

The body lay still—
But a smile touched her face,
As if she heard them say:
"May she find a better place."

She whispered to the sky,
"Let my senses soon be blurred;
If not this life, then maybe next,
Let peace be my final word."

Just One Embrace

Musical chairs—
Who will get the seat?
Let me be the first,
Before I face defeat.

I want first prize,
Not just for me—
But to show my mom
That I, too, can be.

I want to whisper
Soft in her ear:
"I'm your daughter too—
Please call me *dear.*"

See how I'm twirling?
I can soar so high—
Just hug me once tight,
I also want to sigh.

Musical chairs—
Who will take the place?
I'm waiting for her love,
For one warm embrace.

The Voice of God

They looked at her neatly—
But her wounds ran deep.
Her eyes were swollen black,
As if she'd forgotten sleep.

"I sent a beautiful baby
To this place called Earth.
I chose her family,
Believing they'd see her worth."

"I thought I'd done well—
Creating humankind.
I gave them bodies and hearts,
But left compassion behind."

"Have they all become
Machines in disguise?
Why can't they feel her pain,
Or see with human eyes?"

"I must do something
To put an end to this sin.
A world without humanity
Should never begin."

"I'll take a new birth—
And shake them awake.
If they don't change,
It's all I'll take."

Still Me

"If they've ignored you,
Why do you still care?
Don't you have self-respect,
Or did you leave it somewhere?"

That was the question
I asked time and again.
But I know my heart—
It still plays the fool in pain.

I'm an emotional soul,
I don't erase connections.
If they're in trouble,
I forget all past lessons.

In this wide-spread world,
I began with only two.
Not sure what changed—
What tore us through and through.

Maybe they have three kids now,
And options they can choose.
But I had just one parent set—
No one else to lose.

My heart smiled softly,
But didn't call me a fool.
It thanked me instead,
For not bending to the world's rule.

Ink of My Own

Say, "You have to do it"—
Accept who you are.
Grow just a little,
Even if the moon feels far.

Don't look behind,
You've already walked that way.
Pick up your pieces,
And trust your own equation each day.

Everyone was a stranger
When you stepped on this land.
Now your heart seeks just one thing—
Your own joy, close at hand.

If the tears start falling,
Let them come without shame.
Wipe them with your own strength—
Don't wait for others to name.

Grab a blank paper,
And start your own song.
Stand tall like a warrior,
As if glory's been yours all along.

Dear Life

Dear life,
I'm not quite sure—
If I want to live you fully,
Or lose you for sure.

Dear life,
I love you a lot.
I'm giving my best—
Whether you see it or not.

Dear life,
You've seen my highs and lows.
You know how many times
I've worn different clothes of roles.

Dear life,
You're nothing if not bold.
Before I end one chapter,
The next one unfolds untold.

Dear life,
Here's the part I adore:
When the world turns its back,
You're still there—at my core.

From Lost to Life

She did not lose all,
Rather, she found a diamond.
She somehow missed seeing
What would have made her past sweetened.

She found herself
In the mess of the world.
Putting her arms around herself,
She just cuddled.

Said sorry to herself
For not prioritizing herself.
Recognized the fact—
She needs her own help.

Now she has grown up,
Become polite to her own heart.
Now no one can make
Her soul and body depart.

Everyone will see
The shine from her within,
But their praises won't bother—
As she learned to be her own queen.

I Didn't Hear Me

I don't know
What it is—
Is it my fear to lose you,
Or the courage to hold you?

Is it a way toward you,
To feel you from near,
To make a place on the heartshelf,
Or a way away from self?

I do feel you—
Said it to you always.
Did my senses fly like birds
That I didn't hear my own words?

I chased so much
To have a perfect life,
Putting myself in the dustbin,
Treating myself like a machine.

Not angry at anyone,
No blame to others—
I took the wrong route,
But now, I'll grow from sprout.

Scared

Yes, I am scared
to close my eyes,
to breathe too deep,
to hear the cries.

Yes, I am scared
to leave my grind,
to drop the chains,
to free my mind.

I'm scared to face
the girl within,
the broken voice,
the silent twin.

I'm scared to give
her dreams a name,
to light her fire,
to feed her flame.

I'm scared to let
her meet the eyes
of those who fed
her dreams with lies.

Yes, I am scared
to wear a face,
to walk among
this crowded place.

I'm an introvert —
not born, but made,
they cut my wings,
then brought me shade.

But stop this all —
I need to breathe.
I'm scared of meeting you —
I'm scared of losing me.

My scars, Protects You

Every scar has a story —
mine has one too.
Where should I start,
to reveal what's true?

My scars run deep,
they could destroy a lot.
I might find freedom,
but many would be caught in knots.

Should I tell everyone,
from start to end?
Many homes would fall apart —
would I still be called selfish then?

It's better, I think,
you don't ask for my story.
I'm not ashamed —
I'm just guarding your glory.

No grudges in my heart,
no anger in my head.
The crown you wear so proudly,
is tied by a fragile thread.

It's easy to point,
to blame, to shame —
but my silence, dear,
is your life's shade from pain.

So let me live,
with my own solution.
When my truth is known,
God will spark the revolution.

Drawing the Line

I've decided to leave,
to leave everyone behind —
not to run away,
but to treat myself with some kind.

You may forget me,
you may talk behind my back —
but you never realized
your words were real whack.

If I open my mouth,
it'll shatter your pretty look;
you'll find out soon enough
who's the real crook.

When you taunt me,
my heart smiles within,
knowing that the real crime began
from deep within your skin.

Your world would crumble
if I spoke with truth and spine —
the one who gave the scar
was someone once closest to mine.

From the ruins of your broken homes,
I refuse to build mine;
so for your own good,
don't even cross the line.

Painting My Life

It's so beautiful here,
everything feels so new —
finding myself again,
without a single future clue.

I don't know my future,
though small dreams are there;
but today is mine,
the present — real and rare.

Why do we realize all this,
only after such deep pains?
Maybe peace only comes,
once we're soaked by the rains.

I don't want to look back,
or cry on the sad parts;
winning after so many losses —
that's the true art.

I'm enjoying each color,
spread across my palette,
painting my life boldly,
in green, in red, in velvet.

Now, I don't want
anyone else in my story;
may God erase the memories
of my hard-fought, bitter glory.

Sleeping on the Cloud

When I remember those dramas,
I feel like a fool —
on so many silly moments,
I lost my cool.

Those times felt like
an unbreakable trap,
searching for a way out
without a single map.

But now, that struggle
seems so small;
I should've walked straight,
instead of learning to crawl.

Anyway, let's leave behind
all the ifs and buts —
maybe I lost some years,
but surviving took guts.

Today, I know clearly
what my soul really needs —
I needed this peace,
not that restless speed.

When I look back at my fight,
I feel so proud;
finally, just as I wished —
I am sleeping on a cloud.